Zip Zero Impact Production

By

Craig Offutt

authorHOUSE™

1663 LIBERTY DRIVE, SUITE 200
BLOOMINGTON, INDIANA 47403
(800) 839-8640
WWW.AUTHORHOUSE.COM

First published by AuthorHouse 08/02/05

ISBN: 1-4184-9974-9 (sc)

Library of Congress Control Number: 2005904283

Printed in the United States of America
Bloomington, Indiana

This book is printed on acid-free paper.

Dedication

**Life is too short for things many of us should do and
fail to do during our short tenure here on earth.
I worked 20 years before recognizing what is truly
important in life. This book is dedicated to my son
Lance whose death, while the most tragic event in
my life, caused me to change forever.**

Table of Contents

Preface

For decades, people have written books intending to provide new concepts to industrial business. Unfortunately, most business books put us all to sleep while the author grins on the back cover as though he invented rocket science.

The ability of a new business concept to sink or swim is its practical application. What makes us unique is how we apply those new concepts or theories to our daily business practices. Business has always been seen as a game, but it has changed over the past few years. Today it is global. So when any local manufacturer plans to compete for high stakes on a long-term basis, their vision must be worldwide. This simple book is a teaching tool for applying proven principles in an ever-changing industrial world.

Read on and discover actual case results that support this approach to manufacturing at the lowest possible cost and instant delivery to the customer. "Ha!" you say, "Who can really do that?"

We call our approach *Z*ero *I*mpact *Production, or ZIP.*

ZIP (Zero Impact Production)

- Optimum design for manufacturing and assembly (yields best industry cost)

- Ordering and manufacturing flow system driven solely by customer demand

- Minimize new investments with little complexity

- Optimize existing assets

Turn the page to find out how we achieved Zero Impact Production, or as one of our favorite Mexican clients says, "Go home and talk to Mr. Pillow." It may lose a little something in the translation, but "go home and sleep on it" ... better business practices lay ahead.

Introduction

Obviously you are reading this book because you are interested, or maybe you're just bored. In either case, I think you will find it entertaining, informative and very useful.

We own a contract-consulting group which we call *"**Design and Manufacturing Consultants," DMC.*** This book is the basis for our consulting process and for how we run and manage our own corporation.

It is not intended to teach concepts of Kanban, MRP, Lean Manufacturing techniques or magical quality system details. It is a book of strategy and methods to become a leader in any type of industry. It is a combination of proven industry disciplines and a few unique approaches when combined, provide a LEADERSHIP BUSINESS PROCESS.

The book is intentionally short, fits easily in your briefcase; and you can start and stop, and not worry about being confused and losing your train of thought. I think most people take way too long to say what they mean, and waste valuable time that could be used to make money or more importantly, have fun.

Companies today have a major issue with deciding what they want to be when "They Grow Up." This inability to provide guidance and real leadership limits the entire organization from truly reaching its absolute potential. Using the guidance from our process, as related in this book, will provide businesses with the insight to be leaders, strategically focused and have a proven process to sustain strategies within the overall organization.

While I believe education is a cornerstone for good business, it is no substitute for mentors. Any good businessman has a Mentor in the closet somewhere. He or she met someone, worked for someone or was affected by a significant emotional event which drove the entrepreneurial instincts to the surface.

All of us have been sitting in an interview and asked why we wanted the job. Society thinks, and overall culture have induced us to say: because I am a team player, or I want to be with a growing company or think I can help. Well, if I didn't need the money, I would go fishing. Isn't that what capitalism is all about?

Chapter One
Let's Dance

Once, while conducting a training session in Mexico, after giving instructions for the ensuing breakout session, I made the comment, "Let's Rock and Roll," obviously meaning, "Let's go to work." The translators in the meeting said, "Let's Dance," and I was shocked to see how much of a mistake I made. The translations obviously had no effect and added no value to the presentation.

The power of language is tremendous. Whatever language business is being conducted in drives the participants to a position of power. If the language is English, then those who normally speak English have a position of power. We will discuss positional power in a later chapter but it basically means that you have the power, just by the evolution of the situation.

Spanish is 30% longer than English. Anyone who learns another language has to mentally translate in his or her native language, thereby slowing down the mental process and creating a position of power. Gringos are really bad about not understanding communications needs and learning a process of communication properly.

Communication is the most important business factor anywhere. You must establish a system when changing from one language to another, or learn to work in each specific language. For most of us, to speak a language fluently enough to provide adequate business communications is not likely unless you're focused only on one foreign language. Even then, it takes a lot of time.

In an attempt to communicate we need to establish a business philosophy that we both understand. If I speak one business language and you speak another, we will need to translate. Business philosophies are strange. Actually, a lot of them were invented to generate hype and sell books. The basic business tools have existed for years. Oh yes, they have improved with technology, but the basics are still the same. So let's get some common understanding now to allow for solid communication. The basis of our systems are derived from the following:

1. What single factor in any product or process determines the ultimate best cost in a given market or industry? *Design*

2. For the shortest cycle, what should drive the process? *Customer Driven Order*

3. Does anyone in the industry have access to technology which a competitor cannot obtain? *Very Few*

So, based on this discussion, anyone can cut costs, make special processes, look for new technologies for production, reduce overhead, and find a new site with cheaper labor. But the ultimate winner over the long haul is **"The Best Design."**

This book focuses on a system from product concept to production. When using techniques generally available to all industries, and applying the best approach, companies can optimize the lowest cost and will be leaders in their respective markets.

Design, through design for manufacture, works for all parts and process driven products. The system uses statistical methods developed over many years to establish data which can be applied to determine the optimum design.

Design and Manufacturing Consultants, our company, is based on the principles and simple cost-accounting methods to develop competitive product cost. We provide this service to any market and have the ability to compare two or more products of different competitors and get the resulting design cost difference within 3% accuracy. The actual costs may not be within that level of accuracy unless site costs and volume leverages are factored in.

Application of DFM (*Design for Manufacture)* is easily taught and applied. DFA Software was developed for DFM when the time-based system, MTM, was developed for use in industrial engineering for determining labor applications to a manufacturing process. *DMC* has developed its own software: *ZIP* (Zero Impact Production). It is for design improvements, but more importantly for competitive design analysis (CDA).

This software, combined with a consistent method of application analysis, allows us to project design product cost. Once a design product cost is established we translate it to actual market cost based on actual site of manufacture. This extrapolation is developed based upon site manufacture reviews, labor rates, and development of overhead rates.

The old methods for doing competitive evaluation were based on one producer's ability to project what process his competition was using and whether that had an advantage when compared to his own. This only becomes important when it is rocket science, high technology, or if the production process is very unique.

The importance of design assessment is knowing your competition before designing and investing your money.

You need to know where you need to go in order to leapfrog your competitors. A mistake in strategy at the beginning of a project can basically destroy a company over the long haul.

A client who knew he was in bad shape, from a manufacturer's point of view, called me in. Five years prior, he had invested several hundred million dollars in a new design and manufacturing system. He soon found himself in a very negative product cost position. After reviewing what had transpired, I was amazed that he had not done any real detailed competitive assessments. The methodology used was simply guessing and using rumors to develop requirements, specifications, and features. As a result, the product was over-designed and over-featured in a very competitive market. Now what are the alternatives? It's time to redesign again. But first we'll establish a very thorough competitive assessment.

The failure of organizations to know their competitors tends to be more the rule today as opposed to the exception. The basic tactics of war are focused on knowing the enemy first, rather than developing a plan to overcome them. When in doubt, always assume that your competitors know better. Never provide yourself the advantage unless you are sure that you really possess that advantage. Today, technology is changing at a super high rate of speed. Markets are also changing at that same high rate of speed. Business failures are occurring at that same rate of speed. *Be careful. Make no assumptions. Do competitive design assessment first.*

With the advent of mass retailers (*Circuit City, Home Depot, Wal-Mart, Best Buy, etc.*) the point-of-purchase sales approach has significantly changed. Years ago, you could add value to your product over the competition and know that the sales person could use that value to sell the product on the showroom floor. Today, the point-of-purchase is in mass retail. If you can't see it, smell it, or touch it, then you can't get price for it. Features must be value-driven. Price becomes the controlling factor at the value end of the business, unless you are selling in a niche market and can demand price because of lack of competition.

A perfect example is in appliances. My wife and I went to *Best Buy* to purchase a side-by-side refrigerator. We were buying this for our condo, so we wanted some features, but not top of the line. Sitting on the showroom floor were *Maytag, Whirlpool,* and *General Electric.* They were all approximately 25 cubic feet. First, we opened the doors of the *Whirlpool* and slid the crisper drawers in and out. They did not move smoothly and felt cheap. Then, we opened the door on the *Maytag.* The doors felt loose and the crispers had the same issues. Finally, we opened the door on the *GE.* Man, it felt good. And when you opened the crisper drawers they felt like they were greased. Oh, by the way, not one salesperson showed up during this whole time.

We then looked at the prices. The *Whirlpool* was $1099, the *Maytag* was $1149, and the *GE* was $899 with a $50 mail-in rebate. Guess which one we purchased? The *GE.* Based upon our actual work in the industry, we know that *Whirlpool* and *Maytag* offer hidden advantages, but they provide no value at the point-of-purchase in today's market. It is another New World.

As you will see in the following chapters, the use of tools to accurately project market position and cost may be the most valuable weapon in today's industry. As a number of very bright people have said, "Knowing your enemy is more than half the battle."

Remember … the best design wins.

So now, let's "Rock and Roll."

Chapter Two
Product Differentiation

Each industry has developed methods for differentiating products to separate themselves from their competition. World-class competitors have found methods for differentiating at the latest point in their manufacturing process and limiting the differences to those items that the customer is most likely to interface with. Owning your supplier's technology or having exclusives that limit their ability to leverage their production truly increases the cost of production.

In *The Art of War,* written in 500 BC by Sun-Tzu, he discusses several major issues with positioning a strategy to win. All of this applies today and in the future for business. Let me restate the primary drivers that lead any business in deciding how to do business.

1. Determine what it is you want to be when you grow up. *Know yourself before your competitor.*

2. Determine the actual things that your competitors do; not just what you think they do. *Know your competitor as you know yourself.*

3. Determine what things you do well and what things are not a core technology. *Doing things which are not a company's expertise creates results prepared by amateurs – Bill Gates*

Most corporations need to decide what they want to be when they grow up. Many companies have designed for and dictated to their equipment suppliers for years. They demand exclusivity, patents, intellectual property and ownership, but they have no data to indicate that control of equipment design enhances overall sales. If they truly believe that their supplier's equipment is core technology, then they should purchase or build their own. If not, then they need to develop techniques to differentiate a vendor's equipment with a minimum impact to the manufactured cost, thus utilizing industry volume to reduce their overall equipment costs.

World-class manufacturers have learned the need for production leverage and their need to reduce overall costs in order to compete on a global basis. Listed below are several examples of methods used today to provide product differentiation with a stable platform.

1. Whirlpool today produces about 57% of all the automatic washers on the domestic market. They produce units under *Kenmore* for *Sears, Roper, Whirlpool, KitchenAid,* and *Kmart.* They differentiate the products through console styling, agitators, handles, and controls. All are applied at the last point in the production process. This allows them to get major cost leverage on the 2.8 million units produced annually. Competition does the same.

2. Measuring spoons, produced by the millions, are differentiated purely by graphics and then sold in different approaches. What sells at Wal-Mart as generic, sells as Pampered Chef at double the price, with very few customers grasping the fact that they come from the same manufacturing plant.

3. Bottom mount 19 cubic feet refrigerators are made by *Amana* and purchased by *Whirlpool, Maytag,* and *GE.* They are branded externally and sold at

different price points. The volume is limited, thus all of the companies benefit from the volume leverage.

4. Many thermostats for home heating and cooling are exactly the same from model to model, branded by a label or a plastic cover change.

5. *General Motors* sells numerous models on the same chassis. They have the same engines, same electronics, yet differentiate the cars through styling consistent with the given brand. If there is a niche market, like *Corvette*, then a unique, low volume design is created and priced as such. Price here is not the determining factor. Feature value and style become the over-ruling factors. A *GMC* truck is virtually a twin to a *Chevy* except for minor branding. Yet, there is a market every year for those who only purchase *GMC*.

Coke has brand recognition, like *Kleenex* or *Clorox*. People don't ask for a tissue. They ask for a *Kleenex*. People don't ask for a soda or a pop. They ask for a *Coke*. Product display in this market needs to focus on *brand* sales. Appearance, taste and feel are the things that sell a *brand.*

We need to perceive this as assets of twins. If they are identical, and you remove their clothes, you should not be able to tell the difference. If you put one in a suit and the other in a sports outfit, dye one's hair, add glasses to one, teach one to play the piano and the other to play the trumpet, they become individuals with their own differentiation.

Limit the differentiation to aesthetics.

The appearance of the exterior can be dedicated to a specific brand or need. Shape, styling, colors, selections, and controls can all be unique with minimum effect on production volume leverage. Companies should research appearance, and in particular, customer interface. How does the product interface with its customer? Selections, programming, life costs, capacity, and those things that reduce costs to the system are physical attributes to the customer.

Companies are so focused on technical design and ownership that they are trapped in an age-old paradigm of how to sell more products while their competitors focus more heavily on differentiation. Companies need to focus more on quality, manufactured costs, reliability, and ease of use of their equipment and products.

In summary, the lesson of product differentiation is a hard one to learn. Business 30 years ago was not as concerned about low manufacturing costs because global competition had not yet brought the pressure to overall worldwide costs. Today is different. It will be difficult for any supplier to survive without the use of excellent design and production costs to reduce their total costs.

Equipment only enhances point-of-sale through customer interface. There is no proof in the commercial business of vendors, coolers, freezers, and so on that basic construction or function enhances sales. There is proof, at that point-of-purchase, that the consumer can feel, taste, or see something that will affect his overall preference.

Let me leave you with these two final thoughts for your own interpretation. In *The Art of War,* Sun-Tzu says,

> *"Thus it is said that one who knows the enemy and knows himself will not be endangered in a hundred engagements. One who does not know the enemy, but knows himself, will sometimes be victorious, sometimes meet defeat. One who knows neither the*

> *enemy nor himself will invariably be defeated in every engagement."*

So, as we proceed along the journey of learning ZIP, think basic chassis and controlled differentiation.

Chapter Three
Design Improvement:
The Best Design Wins

We use the term design improvement to define the workshop process under ZIP, whereby we take an existing product, tear it down and load it as a base line to the ZIP process. Once this task is completed we proceed to the redesign process.

During this process, we are trying to determine what level of simplicity the current product concepts can be reduced to before proceeding on to Competitive Design Assessment (CDA). These design improvement sessions allow the teams to brainstorm and learn the attributes of the ZIP software and the power of controlled Design for Manufacture (DFM). This newly learned skill will provide intuition and insight associated with eliminating biases and paradigms when evaluating competitive design.

Here's how the process works:

1. The workshop is usually about 5 days. The first day consists of ZIP training including practical exercises. The balance of the week is laid out as follows:

Design Improvement Workshop

Overview: Through the Use of ZIP and DFM Techniques, This Workshop Provides a Complete Assessment of the Current Product/Prototype, Evaluation of Components and Creates a New DFM Design.

Craig Offutt

REMEMBER: *"The Best Design is the Simplest Design"*

WEEK 1: *Cross Functional Team Directed By DMC Support*

<u>*DAY ONE: 1:00 - 5:00 PM*</u>
- *General Introductions*
- *"ZIP" Applications*
- *Executive Overview & Process*
- *Data Collection & Analysis*
- *Practical Exercises*
- *Assignment of Teams & Begin Teardown*

<u>*DAY TWO: 8:00 AM - 5:00 PM*</u>
- *Familiarization of "ZIP" software*
- *Continue Tear Down and Design Documentation*

<u>*DAY THREE: 8:00 AM - 5:00 PM*</u>
- *Continue Tear Down & Design Documentation*
- *Begin Documentation of Quality & Cost Reductions*
- *Start Redesign Documentation*

<u>*DAY FOUR: 8:00 AM - 5:00 PM*</u>
- *Continue & Finalize Re-design*
- *Prepare Presentation*

<u>*DAY FIVE: 8:00 - 11:00 AM*</u>
- *Presentation to Divisional Management*

WEEK 2: *DMC Support Only*

2. The second day consists of disassembly of the product and loading the process to ZIP. The software will create reports, which outline the base characteristics of a given product shown below. This is the first time in the process that we baseline the existing product. All further improvements or competitive assessment will be compared back to this baseline.

"ZIP" CHARACTERISTICS
Baseline Data

Characteristic	Manufacturer			Manufacturer		
	Sub Sys 1	Sub Sys 2	Total Sub Sys	Sub Sys 1	Sub Sys 2	Total Sub Sys
Part Count:						
• Total Parts						
• Good Parts						
• Design Efficiency	%	%	%	%	%	%
Operations:						
Fastening Operations:						
Total Hours / Unit:						
• Assembly						
• Fabrication						
Assembly Seconds:						

3. Wednesday we begin redesign using the tools of "ZIP." This is where we begin to understand the basics of the organization: **Paradigms and Issues** associated with change. When people begin to redesign something that they own, know, see, feel, touch, and so on, they begin to reveal how little they know about their own markets, global competition and how little real strategic business strategy work they have done. It's the process of ZIP that brings all of this to the top for discussion and provides a basis to use the tools of DFM to reduce product cost and develop the best cost. It is almost impossible to administer this type of workshop from within. You need a "Hired Gun," and you need a good one. As we have discussed and will continue to discuss, strategy work is few and far between.

4. Thursday completes the redesign and begins the process of breaking the new design into categories. The process generates results which we categorize into 3 savings groups:

Quickies: 6 months or less projects, minimum risk ... Let's "Rock and Roll." These projects are freebies because the company can get these regardless of whether they pursue the final project redesign or not.

Mid-Term: projects less than one year, limited risk and good marketing impact. Some of these projects may yield for the existing product and some will yield for the New Baby. They should be separated based on a return on investment based on the time required to introduce the change and its projected life.

Long-Term: projects which should be incorporated in the overall redesign process and may not be obtained for 2-3 years.

Long-term projects establish the first approach for the new ZIP redesign, the first cut at the New Baby. Just remember, under the ZIP process, the New Baby will be redesigned as many as six times. As Albert Einstein said, "The First Design is Never the Simplest."

The team estimates the investment, risk and timing associated with each part of the redesign. They chart the total and begin the process of developing a product strategy by going through the workshop. The purpose here is to allow the results to develop the necessary information to begin actual preparation

of appropriations to obtain   capital
and tooling funds with solid financial data.

Client:
Sub System:
Manufacturer:

Project	Timing	Risk Factor	Annual Volume	Savings Per Unit	Annual Savings	Weighted Savings	Investment	Comments
Materials:								
Sub Total Materials								
Labor:								
Sub Total Labor								
Total Sub System								
Simple Payback								

5. On the last day, we gather together all the information, reduce it to ZIP final comparisons and prepare for the managerial report out. Normally, we are ready by midday Friday and hold the formal report out by having each team report on their area of the specific product. Below illustrates the comparisons between the existing baseline and the new design, usually termed the New Baby.

Craig Offutt

ZIP . . . RE-DESIGN SUMMARY			
Model: ___ Date: ___	Team Assembly: ___	Design Efficiency % ___	
DESIGN FACTOR	BASE MODEL	NEW BABY	COMMENTS
Total Operations			
Total Parts			
Total Good Parts			
Design Efficiency %			
Material Cost			
Labor Cost			
Total Cost			
Net Profit @ Current Volume			
Investment			
Years to Break Even			

The thrust of this initial workshop is teaching an organization the basics of ZIP and the business strategy process. It sets the basis for establishing an implementation team which will head toward a formal Big Picture Redesign while developing the overall ZIP Business Strategy.

The cool thing about this part of the process is that even if you elect not to proceed with a New Baby Design, history shows that the short-term returns will generate 10 to 100 times the amount that it costs for the workshop and implementation. It's a no lost deal! I always tell our clients that they do not need to pay us. Just give me 10% of the first year's projected savings. None have elected to accept my offer, but time goes on.

Applying the ZIP process is like algebra. You need to follow all of the steps and not do any of the math in your head. If you skip steps because it seems too simple, then you are certain to make a mistake. Follow the process and it never fails because it focuses on reducing complexity at the lowest and most cost effective level, "Design."

From a Best Cost position, Lean Manufacturing has one huge flaw. It teaches people how to manage complexity, not focus on its reduction all the way down to the basis of design. Design contributes to 80% of the product cost from an impact point of view, however companies spend the least amount of funds in this category. You can beat up on your suppliers and save 1%, or you can cut wages and save 5%, or you can move to Mexico and reduce your cost 30%. But, if you do an optimum redesign, the potential is 50%.

Design improvement is the core to the following steps in ZIP. Go on to the next chapters and hopefully you will be convinced.

Chapter Four
Competitive Analysis

This may be the most important chapter in the book, and the basis for the development of any competitive business strategy. Competitive design assessment provides and builds a knowledge base that, in most cases, allows you to know your competitors better than most of them know themselves.

In most industries, the technology in manufacturing is not particularly unique. High tech industries, like integrated circuits, are another subject. In the run-of-the-mill manufacturing no one has a significantly unique process that provides them a breakthrough to become the leader (Numero Uno) in the industry. Therefore, trying to project manufacturing processes for costs is generally a waste of time. Processes in this type of business have less than a 3% to 5% impact on the total cost.

I have been involved in so many futile attempts to project competitive costs that it is a joke. Typically, companies get a horde of people (purchasers, manufacturers, engineers, etc.) and buy some product. They gather in a room and take the product apart while each functional area attempts to forecast the associated component costs. Procurement calls for quotes, manufacturing engineers try to project labor and how it is processed and design engineers project future costs and what the component's actual function is.

The results are very inaccurate and take 300 to 500 man-hours away from normal business time. What a joke! Industries waste internal resources on projects when they are not experts. Five hundred man-hours, at average wage, to prepare a financial analysis on product costs of $30 per hour loaded cost, says that for each analysis they spend $15,000. What a circus!

If you make refrigerators and management asked you for a projection and a detailed review of cost for the man-hours to design a new type of refrigerator, you would know exactly what to do. If they came and asked for the process detail to produce the paint used on the outside of the unit, you would call your trusty supplier and get the results. Industry needs to learn what is core technology to the company and what is not. Once this is determined, contract those technologies that are not core to the experts. You will save tons of money and get more accurate results.

Our business is not computers, and we do not intend for it to be. It is not a core competence for us, so we contract experts to handle it. And we get expert results.

So, how do you project competitive costs and be assured of reasonable accuracy? We have developed a system that is a combination of basic technologies that can accurately compare any two competitive products and get a cost result within 3% accuracy.

It is very difficult for an organization to develop a strategy and direction without knowing the competitive market and their competitor's position. The following must occur:

1. Determine actual competitive cost comparisons with your major competitors at a design cost level.

2. Do feature vs. feature value to determine if you are getting margin for your feature cost.

3. Do a price point analysis to determine if you are covering the market and if you are competitively featured at each point.

I know your marketing folks have assured you that they have this subject well in hand and that you should not concern yourself with the details. Over the past five years, we have done many of these types of reviews and let me assure you that in all cases there have been major issues with:

- Not getting margin for a given feature

- Not hitting all the required price points

- Giving features away at a given price point

This situation is like anything else in business. If you don't do a Zero-based review every three years you get into real problems.

I was once involved with a company that did not use Zero-based budgets. No big surprise. Few ever do. So at budget time we went through the normal routine of finance sending out a schedule and copies of historical data (actual vs. current year budget). It was stuff we already had but accounting didn't think anybody looked at it. We handed it out to our managers, reviewed the process with them, and lectured them on the importance of all-cost impacts. They took the information, increased all line items and tacked on an additional 20%, their contingency for when we would tell them it was too high. We rejected their plan and sent it back. Now they were ticked off. They retaliated by cutting something they knew we must have. Why? Because they knew we would need to purchase it anyway.

This feature and price point thing is the same issue. We have a model line up, it hits the market first year and we have problems in sales at various points. So now we add a feature here, change a price point for a certain customer and realign what we have because the dealers don't like the line up in

Seattle. Nobody checked Florida or some other area to see if Seattle is unique.

Two months later, the marketing guy gets promoted and a new young college grad shows up with his bright shiny certificate. Of course he can solve anything. He looks at the line and says it is all screwed up. Nothing is right at any price point. So he drafts a huge computer spreadsheet and completely changes the line to meet what he considers to be a correct profile. He sends it to his boss and gets approval because the boss is sure that all of this detail and spreadsheet stuff must be right.

Out to the market it goes, and the new kid gets a big raise. Then the financials come in for the year and show an increase in product costs, profits are down, SG & A is constant and the president says product cost is too high. Now, who can guess what is next?

Yes, that's right, let's call in manufacturing and technology and start some super duper program to cut $50 million of product cost. So now everyone is working on cost reductions. Procurement calls the suppliers and chews on them, finance changes payables from 30 to 45 days, engineering redesigns and spends tooling dollars, manufacturing cuts people off the line, changes the processes and looks for new materials. The new P & L comes out and profits continue to deteriorate. Someone forgot about increased depreciation. They lack focus on the business, lose new project support, and they are not working based on fact, but fiction. What I have described is a money-saving company and not a profit-making company.

Okay, so what did I just say? By using statistically based Design for Manufacture techniques, any organization can develop a very accurate design cost comparison. For most of us, this defines the market cost position and the basics for product cost, as well as new product development. Once you have developed these comparisons, it is very economical to maintain by updating it annually for new competitive products and financial changes to the industry or your company.

The basis for this analysis is as follows:

1. Each product goes through a teardown and is statistically loaded in the DFM software. The software allows the process to be loaded in a reverse order, so it is not necessary to tear the product down and re-assemble.

2. The teardown is done with the assumption of logical processing, combinations of events that occur simultaneously in process or application.

LOGICAL PROCESSING

Logical processing is a methodology developed by DMC for use with the Design software. Because this software was developed to be used as a means to assess a client's design cost, DMC uses Logical Processing as a means of converting this software for use in competitive analysis.

Finished Parts (painted, porcelain, enamel):

*   Cost the raw part based on size, using its X, Y axis

*   Exclude all finishes from the part (List all finish costs as one line item with all unit requirements)

Welding:

*   Do not count each weld as one fastener. Treat each series of welds in the same plane as one fastening operation.

- When you change the plane or shift the material, you encounter a new fastening operation.

Screws:

- For cost purposes, load in $.01 for each screw, unless it is obvious that a special type fastener is being utilized.

- For client costing, adjust final cost to approximate BOM cost.

Functional Test Time (product testing):

- Load into the software a category for functional testing.

Assemblies:

- If the client refers to a series of components as a sub-assembly, assume that the competitor does the same.

- If the client purchases, assume the competitor does the same.

  Example: Manifold Assembly

Sub-Assemblies:

- Minimize the number of parts in a sub-assembly. The more parts you handle, the more time the software adds.   Example:

1	Porcelain Pan	Adds	6 seconds
2	Raw Part	Adds	6 seconds
2	Porcelain	Adds	6 seconds

Just list the raw part! Remember, we will pick up the finish as one line item!

Software:

- Adjust default table setting for screwing operations from 4 seconds to 1 second.

- Adjust default table setting for welding operations from 4 seconds to 1 second.

Operations:

- Work as many operations as you can the same plane before doing a change of direction. Minimize CDI's!

- Labor costs and overhead rate applications are held constant through this entire phase of the project to develop a true or pure DFM design cost.

- Parts are categorized and then costed. Material can be costed through obtaining quotations and using mechanical techniques of weight, gauges, material types and so on to obtain basic part cost.

- The material and labor costs are added, appropriate overheads are applied, and a comparative design cost difference is found at each specific product level selected.

These costs are very accurate to actual, on a relative difference, not an actual cost at market. They also provide the base design cost difference, unaffected by processing and the real world.

The next step in the process is to move these costs from the world of theory to the world of real life. We cannot proceed to that without learning what attributes most significantly influence the accuracy of projecting an actual competitive product cost from the huge world of unknowns.

Keep in mind that for most products, (unless they are highly process focused like tires, rubber, chemicals, etc.) the processing tends to affect the overall product cost by less than 5%. Basic product design contributes the highest degree of impact, and site production provides the second largest contribution.

To move a product cost from a theoretical level of relevance to actual, we need to develop three things:

1. Actual labor rates, manpower related costs and benefits associated at the location of manufacture.

2. Develop a concept of efficiency for the given site. For instance, sites in Mexico tend to be 20% to 50% less efficient than sites in the United States. Sites in southern United States tend to be 10% less productive than northern operations. This information will be used to interpolate the operations data derived from the actual DFM process and determine actual labor costs.

3. Determine how much burden exists so we can apply it to the total manufacturing cost.

Labor historically can be determined in several fashions. The local bars have been the easiest and most reliable way to obtain actual local wage standards, site visitation and vendors. Wages are no big secret anywhere. Just be careful to check and see if any hidden benefit costs exist such as uniforms, transportation, meals, profit sharing, etc. This is very typical in countries outside the United States. Usually, these types of indirect benefits are common to an area and can be found through any general business discussions.

Efficiency can be found by visiting any company in the area of the competitor's region. Efficiency tends to be regional with very few exceptions. It is not necessary to watch the operators work at the competitor's exact operations.

The real hard part is related to overhead. Because so many factors affect this area, you should build a computer model and load the various site or operation attributes. The basis of this analysis requires a site visit to the region of actual manufacturing. As shown in the competitive site profile, it is necessary to determine the age of the facility, how it was or is to be purchased, and how much equipment is internal. Also determine the equipment's age and types of automation.

MANUFACTURING PROFILE
COOKING PRODUCTS
YEAR XXXX

Manufacturer Site	Products	Brands	Size Sq Ft	Annual Capacity	Actual Util	Hourly Employ	D/L Wage
Company A							
- Seattle, Wa	Stoves, Grills	AA, AB, AAB	50,000	45,000	66%	95	$8.25
- Burbank, Ca	RV Stoves	AA,AC	25,000	33,000	34%	44	$14.25
Company B							
- Newark, NJ	Stoves, Grills	BB, BA, BC	77,000	65,000	58%	133	$16.75
- Burbank, Ca	RV Stoves	BA, BC	15,000	22,000	40%	41	$14.25
Company C							
- Boise, Id	Stoves, Grills,	CC,CA,CD	57,000	81,000	71%	150	$12.92
- SLP, Mex	RV Stoves	CA, CB	23,000	33,000	52%	68	$1.81

In addition, you need a survey of local tax rates for wages, property and any potential abatement. Once all of this information is obtained you can load into your competitor site profile computer model and out pops overhead cost. Based on the relationship of how much overhead dollars exist, relative to how much labor or material dollars are in a given product, the overhead is allocated to one or the other and a percentage rate is developed.

The rate should be applied to material or the labor, whichever has the most stability. Overhead needs a special sensitivity test. It is very much affected by region. For example, in the States, it is not uncommon to see overhead or burden rates at 300% of labor. For similar products in Mexico, because of the difference in wage rates, you would expect to see rates of 850%. A rate calculation is the most flexible approach when doing competitive analysis. It allows for changing of various other parts of the costs and easy application of a new burden cost. So check your burden rate in the same given region to test for corrections. If you do not have a production facility in the same region, then find another non-competitive manufacturer and evaluate his operation. The result will provide a basis for comparison.

We now establish a comparison chart of products shown in the following example:

TOTAL COST & DETAILED MATERIAL COST DIFFERENCES

Manufacturer Manucaturing Location Model Style Brand	Company A Burbank, Ca ABC RV Stove AA	Company B Burbank, Ca BCA RV Stove BB	Company C SLP, Mexico CAB RV Stove CA
GROSS ZIP COST			
MATERIAL			
- Purchased Material	49.98	63.61	54.61
- Fabricated / Finished Material	17.89	13.51	14.48
Total Material	67.87	77.12	69.09
LABOR & BURDEN			
- Assembly	22.31	19.01	2.93
- Fabricated & Finish	5.56	5.88	0.89
Total Labor & Burden	27.87	24.89	3.82
GROSS COST - ZIP	95.74	102.01	72.91

MATERIAL COST DIFF:	Actual	(Unfavorable)	(Unfavorable)
- Chasis Sub System	14.50	(0.48)	(2.70)
		1.26 Manif Decal	(1.03) Grates
		(.53) Grates	(.63) Main Top
		(.73) Main Top	(.44) Bushing
		(.23) Insulation	(.60) Insulation
		(.25) Burner Box	

This chart allows easy comparison of all of the competitive products for material, labor and burden. Material must be adjusted for actual to account for in-bound freight on received materials and application of production materials. These can be applied on a percentage basis and estimated through vendor conversations that supply to the given region.

The above example also allows a quick evaluation of which cost factors are causing your product to have a disadvantage. These disadvantages appear by category. If you have a large material cost difference, design or feature most likely drives its content. You will need to feature-reconcile the work now. Take each of the competitive products and make a chart similar to the following.

TOTAL COST & FEATURE RECONCILED COST

Manufacturer Manucaturing Location Model Style Brand	Company A Burbank, Ca ABC RV Stove AA	Company B Burbank, Ca BCA RV Stove BB	Company C SLP, Mexico CAB RV Stove CA
GROSS ZIP COST			
MATERIAL			
- Purchased Material	49.98	63.61	54.61
- Fabricated / Finished Material	17.89	13.51	14.48
Total Material	67.87	77.12	69.09
LABOR & BURDEN			
- Assembly	22.31	19.01	2.93
- Fabricated & Finish	5.56	5.88	0.89
Total Labor & Burden	27.87	24.89	3.82
GROSS COST - ZIP	95.74	102.01	72.91

FEATURE RECONCILIATION:

- Bulk Packaging	(0.82)		
- Black To White Main Top		(0.13)	
- Ignition			(3.47)
Total Feature Reconciliation	(0.82)	(0.13)	(3.47)
Feature Reconciled Cost	94.92	101.88	69.44

This chart allows you to add or subtract costs to your competitor's product to make it equal to the comparative product. This is the feature-reconciled cost. Now, restate the costs and see how the material costs compare. If they are still too high, then you have a distinct design disadvantage and need to do design improvement work, either through improving your current design or by doing a completely new design. Design improvement to existing designs is usually a short-term answer to material cost problems. Seldom do companies have the ability to derive the best design from existing designs because the existing design has too many constraints to allow a true DFM design and way too many compromises have to be made.

Here is a perfect example. One of our clients asked us to come review a project to an improved delivery system within a vending machine. The client had assembled a team to do the redesign, and had provided the team with very specific guidelines on what they could change within the machine and what they could not change. The team used reasonable concepts leading toward a sound DFM redesign. The problem was that they were limited on what parts they could redesign. Therefore, limiting how they could optimize the system. After discussion, it became apparent that this would necessitate an interim design change to meet some market demands and that a new platform design would be next … a platform design that would provide them the ability to do an optimized design.

Now, by reviewing your position at market with your competition, you can set a new cost target of the design and decide whether you can compete by producing your product at your current site location.

Once, all products are established at the same process and cost we begin to assess each one at their actual site of production. The base analysis provides a relative cost of the actual design, including labor and burden. This allows each client to see their comparable material and labor content as compared to each of their competitors. We then take each product, determine the labor and burden at each competitive manufacturing site and determine what we define as Site Cost Advantages.

Site Cost Advantages sometimes compensate for design losses and many times will increase the overall disadvantage a client may have as compared to the competition. Actual site wages are obtained, usually from local government and regional agencies for the specific site. Overhead rates are much more difficult. Usually we make a tour of the competition, blueprint the manufacturing operation, and then create the burden rate. Once these rates have been developed we apply the information to the ZIP product cost and get our new next level of competitive product cost comparison.

Total manufacturing cost is influenced by two other significant factors:

1. When producing in lower cost countries, usually the supply base changes and more suppliers provide parts from the lowest cost area. Mexico and China are perfect examples. Usually the site source savings are 5% to 10% of the material cost and should be included when costs are developed for site source savings.

2. Procured leverage on components varies from one competitor to another based on their various volumes. Our experience shows that this will usually affect the total cost by 1% or 2% of material costs.

By integrating all of these adjustments, we get a very good actual to design cost comparison for each of the competitors.

The results from the design CDA and the site correlation lead us to the development of a big picture redesign for manufacturing as well as the development of a manufacturing strategy. Both of these steps in ZIP are handled in the following chapter.

CDA provides the basis for knowing your competitor and how the worldwide site production may be impacting your market and product. A simple example:

A former client produced freestanding ranges in the United States and their major competitor produced them in San Luis Potosi, Mexico. The site difference alone created a $35 per unit disadvantage for the client. Therefore, unless the competitive design cost of the competitor is really bad, it is very unlikely they would be allowed to compete without relocating to a low cost manufacturing region. When doing this evaluation, freight comparisons for both finished goods and inbound component freight must be included to get the net difference.

Below is an example of two competitive products and their incremental comparison costs for design and then site relocation:

CDA SUMMARIES: FEATURE & SITE RECONCILED COST

Manufacturer Manucaturing Location Model Style Brand		Company A Burbank, Ca ABC RV Stove AA	Company B Burbank, Ca BCA RV Stove BB	Company C SLP, Mexico CAB RV Stove CA
GROSS ZIP FEATURE RECONCILED				
- Material		67.05	76.99	62.62
- Labor		27.87	24.89	30.89
Total F/R Cost		94.92	101.88	93.51
ZIP Hours		0.40	0.36	0.44
Fully Loaded (L&OH) Rate		69.68	69.68	69.68
Site Fully Loaded Rate		Same	72.19	26.70
Site Fully Loaded Labor		Same	25.99	11.75
Site Material Adjustment:				
- Site Relocation		N/A	N/A	(5.00)
- Joint Venture		N/A	N/A	(1.85)
Freight Premium		N/A	N/A	2.50
Projected Site Cost		94.92	102.98	70.02

You will notice from the insert that freight becomes the negative factor and controls the basis of relocation. If the products are large, then a Mexican site near the border is preferable. If the products are denser, then an interior Mexican site is the best choice. Mexican labor at the border is in hard competition and there is some distinct labor unrest. The interior tends to be more stable. If the labor content is really high and the product ships at a high density, then China may very well be the optimum choice. Always remember, when moving to Mexico the rates are 10 to 1 when compared to China's rates. In any case, this system allows you to evaluate those alternatives and to structure overall net cost savings.

Site costs also include the actual labor rates and use a projection of the estimated overhead. We express labor in fully burdened terms. In other words, a fully loaded labor rate for a given project is the base direct labor plus the total variable and fixed burden stated on a cost per hour basis. Assuming no significant change in volumes, this allows us to use the rate based on the hours generated from the competitive design assessment. Once the base assessment is done and we have calculated the actual site cost, then we apply the projected labor rate for that given site.

The point is, treat this like algebra. Do all of the steps and do not skip any so that it prevents errors and provides a basis for determining where the actual savings come from. In summary, when the base CDA comparison is done, we do it using the client's loaded labor rate for all products. Remember the base focus of the process is to focus on the cost of the design. Second, we decide where the actual sites are for the competition so that we can develop estimated burden rates for those sites. We then apply them individually to the products so we can see how it affects the actual competitive cost. Along with the application of projected competitive rates we must add any offsetting inbound or outbound freight which negatively or positively affects the related product cost, as compared to the client.

Next, we consider procured part leverage. If it is thought that the competitor, due to size or volume of purchases, commands a lower cost, then that should be applied to the projected site cost. For example, if we were comparing a small independent car manufacturer to General Motors, we would probably project as much as a 5% factor that GM purchases at lower prices than the small independent guy.

If the client is located in the United States and the competitor is located in Mexico, then we would also apply a labor productivity loss due to the Mexican labor environment. Depending upon where you are located in Mexico determines how much of a loss factor will be used. It normally ranges from 25% to 50%.

If a producer is manufacturing in a low cost region, then it is logical that they are buying materials at a lower cost from their local sources, as opposed to the cost when they were in a high cost region. In Mexico those site source savings, as we call them, range between 5% and 10% of the total purchased material. These estimates need to be applied to the cost comparisons in this step.

When doing CDA, always assume the advantage belongs to the competitor, not to your own product. When in doubt, always give the edge to the competitive unit. This will ensure that you set your target at the lowest competitive level.

Competitive Design Assessment

Overview: This procedure provides competitive design and features reconciled costs for current product and selected competitor. In addition, current BOM's are reconciled to actual, as well as development of potential cost reductions.

Weeks 1-3

- *Tear down of client products*

- *Documentation of materials and labor process*

- *Enter data into ZIP software*

Weeks 4-8

- *Tear down of competitor products*

- *Documentation of materials and labor process*

- *Development of material costs*

- *Enter data into ZIP software*

Weeks 9-10

- *Compilation of data*

- *Reconciliation of data*

- *Development of presentation*

Timing: Ten weeks have been allotted for each platform.

The actual time may vary depending on the number of units selected.

Chapter Five
Business Plan

I discussed making hard decisions in the previous chapter. Making decisions without communication is the next failure. So now that we have the data, we know where our disadvantages exist. We have made hard decisions on site location, redesign issues, cost reductions, layoffs and so on. We need to start the managerial work. We need a plan. This plan is our communication of the vision, strategies, and decisions in a finite way.

With product life cycles beginning to fall below four years, I might suggest that a two- or three-year business plan is far-reaching. If your business is stagnant, that is your fault, because you must not have any true competitors. So three years is probably the optimum approach. A million consultants provide facilitation for business plans. Software exists to do business plans. So do not pay a lot of money to get the plan. You have already done the hard work making the decisions and strategies.

Never allow anyone who is involved in the entire business to contribute. It's human nature to work things in your favor. If you have two plants and the plant managers help with the business plan, then you will get two biased inputs and the stronger of the two will put the biggest slant on the package. In most cases, your safest bet is to use a contract resource that has nothing to gain, other than getting paid, and will execute what it is that you want. Do not pay a lot of money for these resources. There are a lot of good consultants that can help facilitate the plan to completion. Now, if you need competitive analysis work and strategy development, that is another story. Very few people are truly strategic thinkers.

They get overly involved in details and don't think of the ultimate concept regardless of related business aspects.

I was involved with trying to correct a basic product design on a global product. The design had been revised over a period of seven years and still had not gone to market. The product was to be produced in Mexico and most of the production would be consumed in Mexico, although the design would export to the United States, Caribbean, South America and other areas. The cost of the design was too high. The investment to produce was too high. And the product had been pushed around for seven years without managing it to an acceptable financial return. Obviously, there was a high percentage of Mexicans in the group. Both the basic design concepts and manufacturing systems proposed were primarily Mexican technology. The Mexicans had been losing market share with their existing product and needed a new World Class platform to replace their existing product lines.

My career and company have a huge background of major project management, and in this case, that particular industry. One of the executives familiar with our work called me and asked if we would be interested in getting this project to an acceptable financial return. The executive was on the gringo side of the business, but he was looking to import lower cost product from Mexico to help the total financial condition in the States.

We reviewed the project and the financials and found that the whole project had been based on the Mexicans wanting to have a new platform not based on a business strategy. They had not done good competitive analysis and really did not know at what level they would need to compete. Nor did they know what features were needed or how they currently compared at the various price points. These guys had a very complex new design, some unknown features, no comparative data and a very automated, complex, manufacturing proposal.

First, we developed a complete competitive assessment. We knew the product costs and designs in all segments of the competitive market. We reviewed how to do competitive design assessment in the previous chapters. Like we said, you have to know your enemy first before you can develop a business plan. It's just like in sports where the team gets together to watch tapes of their opponents play and then develops a game plan on how they will compete in the game.

Next, we hired a very good Latin American marketing expert and did a price point feature analysis. A price point analysis compares a product at each price range by determining the given features of each competitive product and then comparing those features to your own selected product in that price range. Feature content should be equivalent or you should be getting price for any additions. Below is an example of how to format a price point analysis:

PRICE POINT ANALYSIS
GAS COOKER MODEL COST BUILDUP

Model Number	Feature Description	Delete	Delta	Add	Standard Cost	Selling Price	Delta
BASE MODEL: ABC1000WO							
- (3) 6 " Coils	3/1 Std Speed Coil Elem						
- (1) 8 " Coil	Chrome Combo Pans						
- Standard Speed	Steel Door W/O Window						
- Steel Door	Steel Handle						
- No Window	T'Stat & Selector Switch						
- Non Pyro	2 Indicator Lights						
	Porcelain Burner Box						
	Hinged Cooktop						
	Black Console Assembly						
	No Oven Light						
	Total				$170.27	$220.14	$49.87
ABC1001WO							
- (3) 6 " Coils	Steel Door Without Window	(16.24)					
- (1) 8 " Coil	Black Glass Door W/O/W			19.85			
- Standard Speed	Cooktop Bumper	(0.04)		0.08			
- No Window							
- Non Pyro							
- Steel Door To							
Glass Door							
	Total	(16.28)		19.93	$173.92	$223.20	$49.28
			3.65			$3.06	(0.59)
ABC1002WO							
- (3) 6 " Coils	Black Console Assembly	(27.15)					
- (1) 8 " Coil	White Console Assembly			27.65			
- Standard Speed	Black Glass Door W/O/W	(19.85)					
- No Window	White Glass Door W/O/W			29.88			
- Non Pyro							
- Steel Door Tp							
- Glass Door							
- Control							
- Color							
	Total	(47.00)		57.53	$184.45	$234.36	$49.91
			10.53			$11.16	0.63

When looking at a price point analysis, you should be able to see that you have at least equivalent features and that you are the lowest in cost in a given price range. If not, then you need to evaluate what is causing you not to be the low cost producer.

Immediately following the price point analysis, we did a feature value analysis. In a feature value analysis you select several competitive units or products and compare the actual cost and design of the feature. Once this is complete, you can easily check for the lowest cost approach to a feature or function and use the best one on your product.

FEATURES: Refrigeration

		Product X		Product Y		Product Z	
Exterior	**P/D**	**Feature**	**Cost**	**Feature**	**Cost**	**Feature**	**Cost**
Handles	S	2, 3 Point	4.39	1 Pc, Ping, 3 Screws	3.74	3 Pc, Ping, 3 Screws	3.07
Hinges	D	Upper W/Cover, Center Plastic, Lwr Big Mtl Hinge Cups	1.64	Upper Color Matched, Center Sep Stop, Lower Color Matched	1.06	Upper W/Cover, Center Painted W/Stop, Lower 1 Pc, Plastic Hinge Cups	1.18
Kickplate	D	Full Color Matched	0.90	Small 1 Pc Color Matched	0.61	Small, 1 Pc, Color Matched, Not Installed	0.59
Screw Covers	D	Mullion & Paint Riv		Yes	0.02	None	
Corner Caps	D	Full Color Matched	0.05	New, 2 Snap	0.02	New, 2 Snap	0.02
Door Opening	D	200 Degrees	N/A	150 Degrees	N/A	150 Degrees	N/A
Doors	D	Post Paint, Wool Non Foam In Place, 2" Thick	21.83	Foam In Place, 2", Pre Paint, Lance Corner, Snap In Gasket	21.03	Full Foam In Place, Pre Paint, Lance Corners, Snap In Gasket, Carved	26.16
TOTAL EXTERIOR			**27.81**		**24.48**		**30.02**
Structure & Function		**Feature**		**Feature**		**Feature**	
Cabinet	D	Pwdr Coat Blanks	20.27	Pre Paint	17.99	Pre Painted, Lock Corner	22.30
Cabinet Foam	D		15.01		12.90		12.86
Back Panel	D	Pre Paint, Primed, Side Insert	3.14	1 Pc Prime Pre Paint	2.38	Galvanized	1.92
Bottom Panel	D	Part of Back	0.00	Part Of Back	0.00	Part of Back	0.00
Compressor	D	Embraco	33.76		30.64		36.77
Motion	D	Post Paint, 6 Rivets, 17-Brackets	0.53	Pre Paint	0.53	Pre Painted, 6 Screws	0.60
Lights/Fresh Food	F	Top W/W Cover	0.59	2 W/Plastic Guard	1.42	Top W, No Cover	0.57
Lights/Freezer	F	None	N/A	1 Covered	1.87	No	N/A
Cubic Ft		18.6		17.0		18.2	
Power Cord Exposed Length		64" Part Of Harness	N/A	71"	N/A	67"	N/A
Controls	P/D	Cheat Knobs, FF & FZ	9.86	Dual / Electromechanical	11.27	Single Therm Organic	13.51
Warranty		1 Yr P/L, 5 Yr Sealed	N/A	1 Yr P/L, 5 Yr Sealed	N/A	1 Yr P/L, 5 Yr Sealed	N/A
Energy			N/A	478 KWH	N/A	479 KWH	N/A
TOTAL STRUCTURE & FUNCTION			**83.63**		**78.90**		**88.38**
Internal		**Feature**		**Feature**		**Feature**	
Fresh Food Moveable Shelf	F	3 Split Catcher Slide In, Glass	11.02	3-1/2 Glass, Spillproof	12.06	4 Full Glass, Spillproof	12.51
Freezer Shelves	F	1 Full Wire	1.03	1 Full Wire	1.84	1 Full Wire	1.50
Crispers & Crisper Shelves	F	3, Manual Humidity, 1 W/Seal	15.58	3, Manual Humidity, No Seals, Glass Top	14.33	3, Manual Humidity, No Seals, Glass Top	14.40
Deli Pan	F	1 Pc	1.41	Clear, Glass Top	1.51	1 Pc	1.92
Dairy	F	1/2 Clear	0.86	Clear, Partial	1.12	Full Clear	0.72
Butter Tray	F	No	N/A	No	N/A	No	N/A
Mounting:							
- Fresh Food Compartment	D	Slide In	N/A	3 Bar Cantilever	1.27	Slide In	N/A
- Fresh Food Inner Door	F	Molded, Snap On Fronts	2.89	Pickoff	4.35	Molded, Snap On Fronts	2.33
- Freezer Compartment	F	Vacuum W Pub Ins	N/A	Pop In	N/A	Pop In	N/A
- Freezer Inner Door	F	2 Snap Front Trim	1.38	Pickoff, Pin Down	5.50	Molded, Snap On Fronts	1.36
Ice Tray	F	2 Mini Opening	0.56	Ice Maker/Compat	7.51	2 Mini	6.47
Bottle Retainer	F	No	N/A	Stringers	0.20	No	N/A
Egg Tray	F	1 Handle 14 Count	0.50	No	N/A	No	N/A
Ice Pan	F	Yes	0.80	Yes	1.09	No	N/A
TOTAL INTERNAL			**40.12**		**71.06**		**34.84**
TOTAL FEATURES			**151.46**		**174.44**		**153.24**
Feature			54.33		85.99		50.84
Design			97.13		88.45		102.40
Feature Reconcile Adj					(31.66)		3.49
Exterior			25.22		22.77		26.23
Structure & Function			10.83		14.46		13.93
Internal			18.20		48.76		8.68
Total			54.33		85.99		50.84

Next we drafted a competitive strategy and presented the results within the total business. What happened??? Well, the normal managerial response (notice I said managerial not leadership) was that everyone wanted to focus on small individual issues within the strategy, focusing on how much better the business case for the new product now looked. We had provided them a complete strategy for the total business with alternatives to reach number one or two in the industry. They wanted to discuss the redesigned, seven-year project and how we fixed it. We left them with the strategy, went away and applied it to their so-loved new product and returned to explain it differently. Amazingly, they could not understand what to do and hired us to take the project to basically a release to do it phase. There is an end to this Mexican soap opera, but you will have to read on to find out.

The point here is those business plans and strategies help drive leadership instincts–not managerial instincts. In today's business the culture of leadership has been destroyed. We do not train people to become leaders. We train people to be managers, to manage complexity and assign and develop business procedures to control people and clients. We did not teach them to think strategically. We did not structure their income and bonuses based on leadership, leading to control of profit and income. We screwed them up. We taught them to control people and issues. Not that it is not needed, but someone has to provide the Vision, the Direction and the Where we are going. That's the business plan with some finite numbers and words that are specific about what is to be done. No generic statements that say we will get bigger by being better than our competitors. What does that mean?

A strategy will establish numbers like: 3% market share growth through the development of a new feature, or 10% increase in net profit due to the elimination of eight supervisors and six engineers. Be real specific if you want to lead. If your mission and direction is foggy, then your people will get lost in the fog. Be clear and provide vision for all to see and contribute. Also, if you are strategic in nature and tend to be a leader, do not forget to look over your shoulder once in a while to see if the gang is still following you. Sometimes they do not think as fast as you or maybe you gave weak directions and they got lost. So check the status once in a while.

Once your market position is established from factual information, you have developed a vision or direction and have been perfectly clear about what is to be done, you can step into the world of implementation. Marketing releases and definitions, manufacturing strategies, product launch plans, feature development and, last but not least, cost control. Now we are into the real managerial issues and this is the point where you establish a process and the methods to control it.

Each functional area now needs to respond to the vision, the numbers that we have so dearly developed and want. A group meeting is required with the leaders of each of the functional areas. The CEO must be perfectly clear about what he is proposing as the vision and very specific about meeting the numbers. Allow them one week to develop their plans independent of each other. Tell them that they should use DFM, Design For Manufacture, techniques to develop the simplest approach and design. They will have a brain freeze. The marketing guy will say he does not understand how design techniques fit his business. His business is an art based on research, focus group responses, demographic studies and so forth. Well here we are again trying to teach managers to be leaders. These responses are managerial issues, not leadership issues. Our old saying is, "These guys and gals are just like birds with lead in their butts; flapping their wings with no hope of flight." They have to learn to fly. What you want is a plan. What they think you are asking for is the implementation detail. That all comes later. Right now, everyone needs to get in the same ballpark.

The best example of this is a story about a freestanding range manufacturer. The manufacturer developed a new product design for manufacture techniques but by using a design team led without a fixed process. They selected a team leader with a very one-dimensional functional area background: engineering. They did develop a charter with target costs and other general product specifications. Market research was performed and integrated within the total project, mostly based on features and appearance. The competitive work done was minimal and so actual costing was poor. The design team went through a number of test failures during development and continued to add parts and cost along the way. The product went to production and was a huge success at market level. Profits were down. The organization struggled to make cost reductions hoping to improve margins. Competitive pricing continued to drop. Margins and earnings continued to slump. Market share increased and floor exposure continued to improve but profit sucked. Within two years we were asked to analyze the business and develop competitive assessment. We did! It was amazing. Their market position work was so poor that within two years this product had a 12% cost disadvantage to the lowest cost producer while the design met market and feature needs and increased share profits plummeted. Why? They did not develop a market position, had no real price point analysis and used a plan based on opinion and poor data. What are we in the business to accomplish? Profit is the answer. You can have the prettiest design in the business, but if it is not competitive you eventually lose. Treat the competitor as if they have all the advantages as well as the best cost. This challenges the organization to yield longer-term solutions and know what to project.

Our approach to business strategy integrates the CDA and site data on the front end of the strategy development. A team needs to be selected to help develop the strategy and should be cross-functional in nature. Participants should include: marketing, sales, manufacturing engineering, design engineering, and finance and should have a lead person as the coordinator. The participants should be of significant level in the organization to be able to make real decisions or need to be empowered to make real decisions for the particular function that they represent. The following shows the development process for business strategy.

The Business Strategy Process ..."ZIP"

'ZIP' ... Zero Impact Production

In the first session of the strategy development we begin by familiarizing the strategy team with the CDA and site evaluation information. Next, we divide the group into smaller groups and have them develop an objective of the strategy. Basically, "What do you want to be when you grow up?" Once the groups have developed their objective we regroup and discuss them until we reach consensus on the objective. The objectives need to be time bound and measurable. One of our clients, who elected to do the entire ZIP process starting with CDA and going all the way to actual production, developed one of the soundest objectives. They were manufacturing cooking products and said the following:

We will be a full-line supplier and will rank in the number three position in the industry, driving a net margin annually of 15%, within three years of the start of the strategy implementation.

This example is simple, time-bound and measurable.

Once this mission is agreed upon, then the team can focus on next steps to the business plan. The next steps involve developing a marketing Wish List. It is a brainstorming session allowing the sales folks, along with the team, to ask for anything they want for their product. Remember, business plans are strategic and the marketing needs are incredibly important. They need to be stretch features, concepts and ideas that drive you ahead of the pack as well as put some realism into the plan. No, they will not all happen and some will change. But, they act as a holding card in the plan.

Next, we train the team to do a Big Picture Re-Design.

Chapter Six
Beginning Execution

Here we are getting ready to take some of this high-class data and do something with it. The next step is to drive the business plan into a manufacturing strategy. Manufacturing strategy development must be focused in two ways. One is to decide what kind of manufacturing philosophy best fits your overall business. We teach Lean Manufacturing Techniques. Lean Manufacturing has been called the Toyota Manufacturing Methods, JIT, Demand Flow Technology and many other names. It is basically pull manufacturing based on build-to-order concepts with optimization of both human and capital resources. We use Lean because it focuses on utilization of existing assets, minimal automation and related speed to market concepts.

During this phase, we begin by taking the overall philosophies and turning them into a Factory Master Plan, which is used to direct an implementation team through the execution.

The Factory Master Plan will include not only equipment and tooling plans but the plans to meet the operational directives of a manufacturing operation such as: inventory turns, finished goods inventory, total product cycle time needs, scheduling plans, capacity requirements, etc. The insert below shows an example of these operational objectives and what a lean type manufacturing approach might be for a given set of objectives.

Company XYZ   *Factory Master Plan*

<u>*Measurements*</u>

Measurement	2002	2003	2004	Annual Change
- Hours / Unit	10.8	9.0	7.0	10%
- Scrap				
* Gross Scrap / Unit	$15.88	$12.30	$9.60	40%
* Net Scrap / Unit	$11.53	$9.17	$8.42	27%
- Hourly Wage Rate				
* Direct Labor	$9.20	$9.48	$9.76	3%
* Skilled Trades	$15.00	$15.45	$15.91	3%
* Benefit Percentage	43%	43%	43%	N/C
- Conversion $ / Unit	$85.22	$80.96	$76.91	5%
- Units Produced / Employee				
* Total Employees	80	91	115	44%
* Manufacturing Employees	100	105	145	45%
- FG Inventory Days	27 Days	25 Days	19 Days	30%
- WIP Inventory Days	16 Days	13 Days	8 Days	50%
- RM Inventory Days	10 Days	8 Days	7 Days	30%
- Total Product Cycle Time	5 Days	3 Days	1 Day	80%
- Complexity				
* # Of SKU's	1655	1322	1101	33%
* Avg # Parts	1222	1175	1002	18%

You will notice that the parameters are very definitive and time-bound associated to when the expected results will occur. This provides the implementation team with the required deliverables for how they will specify equipment and how assembly and the required support systems will be designed and specified.

In conjunction with the manufacturing implementation team efforts, a cross-functional new product design team for the new "ZIP" product design must be established. This team will include marketing, industrial design, product engineering, materials, logistics, production management and the manufacturing implementation team. This implementation team will take the Big Picture Re-Design details provided by the executives and now drive it to a detailed design level. Actual prototypes and tooling projections are made. In conjunction with the implementation team, they will develop investment costs and build the Factory Master Plan. This plan will be all-inclusive covering new product needs and maintenance of the business items such as roof repairs, new office equipment, etc. In addition, all other facets of the business will be addressed from market and advertising needs all the way down to supporting the current product and requirements.

Shown below is a typical category of the Factory Master Plan … New Product Development Plan. Most of the time in the recent decade, these Factory Plans are projected over three years and updated annually based on business and economic changes or new product development. By no means are they stagnant. They become the living strategy documents which can flexibly change without changing business needs.

Company XYZ   *Factory Master Plan*

Investment Detail … New Product Development

Project Name	Approved / Budget ($000)				Cash Flow Spending($000)			
	2002	2003	2004	Total	2002	2003	2004	Total
Name of Project								
- Capital Equipment	100	50	27	177	50	100	27	177
- Procured Tooling	40	10	5	55	25	25	5	55
- Make Tooling	3	0	0	3	3	0	0	3
- Temporary Tooling	2	2	0	4	2	2	0	4
Total	145	62	32	239	80	127	32	239

Description of Project Strategies
Cost savings $ / Unit
Years to Payback
ROI

These plans are critical to successful product introduction and focus the entire operations organization on the task at hand. Thus, they improve the use of monetary and people assets toward the same goal and direction. Below is another insert providing an example of what maintenance of the business project sheet might resemble. The items are clear and definitive. So even if your organization changes frequently, the next generation of employees can follow the "Cookie Trail" left behind.

Company XYZ   *Factory Master Plan*
Investment Detail ... Maintenance of Business

Project Name	Approved / Budget ($000)				Cash Flow Spending($000)			
	2002	2003	2004	Total	2002	2003	2004	Total
- Safety Upgrades	25	15	4	44	25	15	4	44
- Resurface Parking Lots	0	15	5	20	0	15	5	20
- Press #5 Repair	0	19	0	19	0	19	0	19
- Remodel Office	0	0	22	22	0	0	22	22
Total	25	49	31	105	25	49	31	105

Detailed Description Of All Projects

In the following few pages, we have developed an actual Factory Master Plan for a hypothetical company, XYZ Company:

1. Objective and Projections

2. Big Picture Re-Design and Project Charter

3. Manpower Projections: Direct and Indirect

4. Volume Plans by Product

5. Capacity Charts and Bottlenecks

6. Investment Plans by Category and Product Descriptions

7. Cashflows

8. IRR and Project Financial Sensitivity

9. Factory Plan Projections

If multiple operations are involved in the project then the overall business plan must cover all manufacturing locations first. Then each division must develop individual strategy plans for their location which meet the overall strategy plan.

These types of strategies become much more complex due to each individual location having its own specific agenda. When multiple locations are involved a coordinator must control their contribution to the total strategy.

Once the Factory Master Plan is developed and agreed to by management, then the true implementation begins. The cross-functional design team developed in the beginning now transfers responsibility to the implementation team, which is comprised of the cross-functional groups: day-to-day engineering, manufacturing engineering, quality, cost accounting, manufacturing and other functions directly related to operations.

A project leader in this mode must possess a multifunctional background that will allow him to know when a project is floundering and when members of the team are not performing as required, unless you like to fail to meet objectives. A lot of bullshit goes on in a company and a lot of Bull Shitters have managed to stay employed for a number of years. So be careful whom you select to head the group or you will meet with disaster. The team leader must be dynamic and be allowed to assert his authority and must be given "Positional Power" by the highest-level manager at the site. Now we are looking for timely and low-risk execution. Too many politics or too many levels will bring the project to its knees. At this point, everyone should have approved the design and approach. If a new guy or gal hits the scene, bring them up to date. But short of a major screw-up, the new guy has to buy in and support the ongoing directive.

During execution there are numerous checkpoints which need to be followed. In the execution mode remember that we are designing all parts of the plant and product. We call this system coordination, New Model Planning, of which there is a new model planner or planners. This job is absolutely the cornerstone, second only to the team leader, for success or failure. In most situations the new model planner tracks the entire product in a part-by-part mode from design conception to actual production. Below is an example of part by part. As you will note, each part within the final product is listed by number and by any given model. The planner will check to see that engineering released it on time, that procurement got quotes, that cost accounting loaded the cost, that manufacturing released the tooling, that the design laboratory approved the design, etc.

Company XYZ
New Model planning
Part - By - Part

| Part # | | Supplier | Lead | Part Release | | PO.Rtr | Sample Approval | | Eng | 1st Part |
ECN #	Desc	Usage	Time Wk	Request	Actual	Com Cd	Orig Dt	Actual	Buyer	Approval
832188	Relay	XX Co								
		2	6	2-Nov				15-Nov	Jones	
552122	motor	XO Co								
		1	15	8-Nov				22-Nov	Mayer	

The major events within the schedule are as follows:

1. Engineering design release: The point at which engineering releases a drawing to the operation to be acted upon, either by procurement or by manufacturing.

2. Procurement release: The point at which a vendor and tool has been selected and a purchase order loaded.

3. Manufacturing release for tooling: The point at which a make part has tooling estimates, is reviewed for design for manufacturing and is ready to release for final tooling.

4. Design revisions: All design inevitably requires a change along the way. Each change must be evaluated for schedule, investment and product cost impact.

5. Engineering Bill of Materials release: This varies with each individual company, but each company must decide when they want the engineering BOM to become real and control the operation. The BOM drives accuracy and the background to control the final product and must be accurate and controlled.

6. Manufacturing Process approval: For each part there must be a point where the process to produce the part is approved for use. This is controlled by using capability and design review with the implementation team.

7. Pre-Pilot: At this point we are ready to build a few products of each type. They can be built from tooled parts, prototype parts, and so on. The sooner we build a few units and check for accuracy, the better. These units are scrap and cannot be sold. They are the first step to product verification prior to production.

8. Pilot Production: Usually 4 to 6 weeks following pre-pilot we have tooled and approved parts of everything. Pilot is the time when you do final verification of the new product. You build a few units, usually 25, of each stock-keeping version of the new product. Build them exactly as the specifications require to verify the overall system and to confirm readiness for actual volume product. These products closely represent what the final production will look like. Therefore, they are usually saleable products even if they require some

minor rework. If the pilot fails to be correct within the existing system then product is delayed until the problems can be corrected and a new pilot is run.

9. Production release: Once a final Pilot is successful, all other system factors are reviewed: processes, tooling, capacity costs, results and performance from Pilot, etc. Usually production will begin 4 to 6 weeks following pilot.

Sounds like a lot of work. It is not too bad if you allow the team to do the "ZIP" process in the beginning and to finitely specify the project charter. The greatest failure to projects comes in the up-front planning stages and not necessarily design. The painful areas are market evaluation, the product specifications, focus group results and market research data analysis.

OK, believe it or not, we are ready to begin design. The planning process is crucial and, as far as I am concerned, without it you are doomed to waste money and resources. Maybe even fail. The next chapter gets on with the design.

Chapter Seven
Design

The design stage is the next crucial step to any successful new product. Using ZIP to control the manufacturability will assure lowest cost. The implementation team should meet on a periodic basis, usually weekly, and discuss how they are performing relative to the established charter. The team should discuss open issues and critical decision points to stay on cost and schedule.

The team leader would review the project status with upper-level management on a monthly basis. As part of this review the team leader should bring a revised charter with the recommended changes to the project if any exist at that time. At the end of the review they should ask for the signatures of the responsible management individuals on the charter to confirm leadership agreement to any project changes since the original inception. While they have sanctioned the team to implement, that does not mean that they have given away the power to control what their function does relative to the overall business. That's what they get paid to do.

As this design progresses through the phases of development, there will be checkpoints, tollgates, for making critical decisions.

1. Design Concept Approval

2. Design Implementation

3. Production Release

4. Market Audit

DESIGN CONCEPT APPROVAL

This phase is probably the most important phase in relating the design to the charter and to the actual market requirements. During this phase the technology group is developing concepts per the sales release and the charter statement. The most critical part is keeping the team focused on the actual requirement. The greatest tendency is to develop a concept that does not meet all of the charter or market needs. For example:

After working with one of our clients for almost nine months we were ready to enter the design phase. Sales releases had been distributed and a team charter developed. The business was based on vending cold drinks. In an attempt to become number one in the industry there were several major factors which needed to be met.

1. Lowest target cost in the industry.

2. Simplicity and standardization.

3. Functionality and reliability.

4. Dispensing of "Things" not limited to cold beverages.

Well, as paradigms would have it, the finest design concepts were heavily focused on dispensing cold beverage cans and bottles and not dispensing things like: golf balls, tennis balls, hose, etc. So that's the issue. As we say, someone with impeccable logic needs to audit the team and when they fall off the road and get in the ditch, he will get them back on the road. This attribute is provided by our firm and can be developed within an organization.

Failure, in this phase, to develop the right concepts to meet the market will surely cause a market introduction failure.

When the concept has been reduced to practice, functioning prototype stage, then a review would be called from all functional areas and a ZIP workshop performed to make sure that the design has been reduced to the simplest approach and therefore the lowest cost approach. In addition, this is the time to make sure it meets the market requirements. Following this phase, we go to the tollgate with management and present the status and results for approval.

Below are two examples of correct and incorrect ZIP strategy designs:

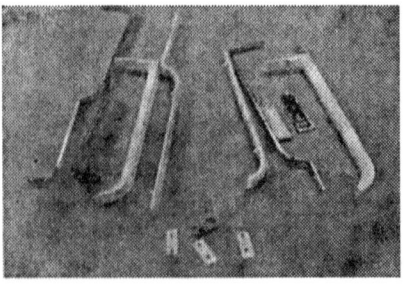 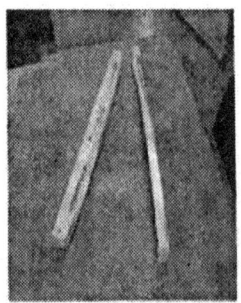

Their two designs compare methods for designing a refrigerator door handle system. The poor design did not utilize ZIP techniques. The good design was a ZIP design and has reduced the number of parts and manufactured cost to the best-cost level.

Using ZIP design methods will reduce the probability of your competition being able to redesign beyond your new product introduction without long lead times. This design issue reduces the complexity of managing the project. The overall tracking of the new product introduction becomes much easier and allows the New Product Planning function to manage fewer issues.

New Model Planning, as described earlier, tracks and manages all of the described dates and is responsible to keep the water flowing downhill at the right rate. When bottlenecks occur, NMP must notify management that the project is failing to meet schedule.

DESIGN IMPLEMENTATION

Once the Concept Design release phase tollgate has been passed we proceed to design implementation. If it fails the tollgate then the schedule is reworked and new concepts and/or revisions must be processed until the tollgate criteria are successfully met. Measuring the design based on Design Efficiency, Good Parts divided by Total Parts will allow the tollgate review to measure the manufacturability of the product and whether the team has focused on the right amount of optimization. Design efficiency percentages should be set immediately following the CDA work, described in earlier chapters, by relating competitive efficiencies to World-Class Design levels and setting your targets significantly above those.

During Design Implementation, procured parts, manufactured parts, equipment, and so on, are being tracked to the New Model Planning schedule based on production data requirements relative to the release of a part and the time to get that part. As a result, the entire design release to production phase-in can be tracked.

Now the team takes the approved concept and begins the design implementation. This means drawing, testing, worst-case design analysis and so forth. Once the design reaches the Design Conformance Stage, samples and design detail is submitted for testing to the required product specifications and reliability requirements. At this phase, the test conformance work is the next tollgate known as Design Conformance and Release for Tooling. Once approved, final tooling release and manufacturing requirements can be implemented.

During this entire process New Model Planning continues the rigorous task of tracking all parts through each of their respective tooling and/or various types of creation: tracking delivery of samples approval of parts to the design specification and releasing early orders for production start-up. Production ramp-up plans vary somewhat based on the complexity of design, but the following insert shows a typical new product introduction plan.

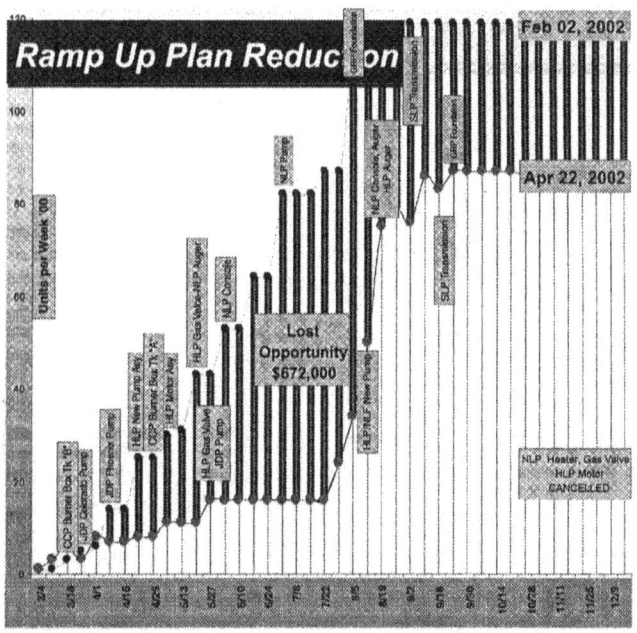

Mexico Part Introduction Ramp Up Plan

			Annual Volume	Pilot Date	12/17	7-Jan	2/18	2/25	3/4	3/11
PPAP	=PPAP									
	=PILOT									
	=PRODUCTION									
ARP	Facade	??	??	??						
ARP	Ice Crusher Bin	??	??	??						
ARP	Machine Compartment	??	??	??						
ARP	Roller Bracket	??	??	??						
CCP	Burner Box Asy Tk A	P189-01	75000	29-Apr						
CCP	Burner Box Asy Tk A	P183-01	60000	27-May			PPAP		250	250
CCP	Burner Box Asy Tk A	P283-02	23000	17-Jun						
CCP	Burner Box Asy Tk A	P226-01	16000	10-Jun						
CCP	Burner Box Asy Tk A	P216-01	11000	11-Jun						
CCP	Burner Box Asy Tk A	P183-03	3000	18-Jun						
CCP	Burner Box Asy Tk A	P217-01	800	12-Jun						
CCP	Burner Box Asy Tk A	P189-02	600	19-Jun						
CCP	Burner Box Asy Tk A	P190-01	600	20-Jun						
CCP	Burner Box Asy Tk A	P283-03	300	13-Jun						
CCP	Burner Box Asy Tk A	P183-02	200	24-Jun						
CCP	Burner Box Asy Tk A	P226-02	200	25-Jun						
CCP	Burner Box Asy Tk B	P282-01 B#3	90000	4-Mar	2P		PPAP		250	250
CCP	Burner Box Asy Tk B	P282-02 B#4	77000	1-Apr						
CCP	Burner Box Asy Tk B	P185-01 B#1	2000	15-Apr						
CCP	Burner Box Asy Tk B	P271-01 B#2	300	29-Apr						
GRP	Fountain Disp Elec	??	226000	6-Aug						
GRP	Fountain Disp Slide	??	111000	5-Aug						
HLP	Gas Valve Asy	53-0737	120500	22-May						
HLP	Motor Assembly	35-5934	874800	6-May						
HLP	Pump Asy (New)	XW025XX	1306220	17-Jun						
JDP	Control Panels	??	??	??						
JDP	Pump (Colorado)	6915958	140000	11-Mar			PPAP		500	
JDP	Pump (Monroe)	??	??	??						
JDP	Pump (Phoenix)	6915237	810000	8-Apr						
JDP	Service Pts (plug in)	??	??	??						
NLP	Atlantis Washer Console	MAV-1/4	452433	23-May	3P					

59

PRODUCTION RELEASE

Before entry into the introduction process the design must pass The Production Release Tollgate. Verification of design, conformance and production readiness is judged at this tollgate. All exceptions are noted, and production is delayed or modified based on the results of this tollgate. Once successfully passing this gate, the production introduction plans begin.

MARKET AUDIT

Once into production a final tollgate, known as Market Audit Tollgate, reviews the success or failures of the introduction, quality of production and any corrective actions needed to improve the performance of the overall product both to design and to the results from the market. During this review production might be stopped or modified to improve quality, reliability and/or make required product revisions to meet changes in the market requirements which were overlooked in the process.

Well, I suppose you're thinking that this is the end of the story: not by a long shot. Now we go back to strategy and enhance the total process. Remember that the world is dynamic and that the guy who is "continually dissatisfied" is the guy who wins. Dynamic strengths and power at market is derived from the desire for change and the ability to implement using ZIP strategies.

Chapter Eight
ZIP Strategy

In the beginning we said, "What do you want to be when you grow up?"

As a result, we need to continue to review the market needs and to review new competitive products and/or revisions to existing products. When a change is detected, a new CDA needs to be contracted to update the competitive product files created in the early stages of the described ZIP process.

Depending on the market changes, product configurations and/or revisions and new needs of your own company, you need to review your strategy. The original answer to the "Grow Up" question may have now changed or will vary somewhat from the original process. For example:

> In the beginning there was a company that produced ballpoint pens. During their original strategy work, they said they wanted to be the highest volume pen manufacturer with a net income of 8%. As a result they established a new design on conventional activities that a ballpoint pen would provide.

> With the introduction of the new design, they gained a new competitor. The new product had a feature which allowed them to gain a significant amount of market share from the manufacturer who had just introduced their new low-cost pen. The new pen provided the feature that when you put it in your pocket, the clip would cause the pen to retract automatically.

While this is a very simple example, no one can be interpretive enough to anticipate particular market breakthroughs and especially invention. Yet, utilizing the ZIP Strategies and approaches to new product development reduces the risk of this kind of failure. The use of CDA to know the competition and focus the team on competitive products, in addition to design simplicity, usually drives the team to the best cost and feature design, thus limiting issues such as the retractable pen breakthrough.

Below is an example of utilizing low-cost labor regions to handle complex components and a modularization of design:

As you can see from the example, in an attempt to optimize product design, they have eliminated the ballast from the light, proceeded to snap together design, and through technology developed an electronic tube firing circuit. The tube, or bulb-firing device, is electric and requires a lot of labor to make. So they have sourced the assembly to a low-cost region of the world, China, and received it back in the U.S. to assemble it to the light.

In general, when evaluating the need for using worldwide regions for products, it should be judged primarily on labor content and size. In using Mexico and China as the prime comparisons, we generally say that if you relocate a product to Mexico you should figure a ten-to-one labor savings. So, if the loaded labor rate discussed earlier is $50 per hour then Mexico would be about $5 per hour. The same situation exists for China and other underdeveloped nations of which we roughly say 100 to 1. While these are not exact ratios and will change as countries develop, they provide a sense of judgment when deciding if products could benefit from relocation.

Next in line is freight. If you have large products, like refrigerators, then producing them as close as possible to the consumption point makes the most sense. Freight can easily absorb the savings if the product is not shippable in a dense format. For large products Mexico obviously makes the most sense. If it is a flashlight, then first reviews should be overseas in a low-cost region.

Product strategies are complex. During the CDA process, you should identify manufacturing locations of competitors, labor rates and contents. This way, when you are reviewing your new product opportunities you can evaluate the potential for non-U.S. production.

Today it is a world economy, not a domestic one, creating pressure to reduce selling prices or maintain them, thus forcing more and more efforts to reduce manufactured costs. We created the situation as consumers by buying the lowest cost products, whether they were U.S. produced or not. So don't go blaming this stuff on the big companies. Start looking in the mirror.

Look at electronics. The majority of these products, televisions, disc players, and so on, are cheaper today and add ten times the features than they did ten years ago. Our failure as Americans is to get too complacent about our status, too lazy to get ahead before other countries trash us. The influx of high-quality and cheaper cars from offshore drove the U.S. to re-engineer the car business. The steel companies went under not only due to competition, but also due to Americans wanting everything "now." We demanded clean air tomorrow. The air did not get screwed up overnight so why do we have to fix it today? Let's begin a process of controlled improvement at a controlled cost where we can still compete in the world.

In development of product strategies, we need to understand that the market is traditional and makes these rash judgments about what it wants without thought to the rest of the world and its related impact on our overall economy. Follow the simple ZIP Strategy steps:

1. Know your competition … CDA.

2. Decide what you want to be when you grow up.

3. Develop a sales release and identify the product needs.

4. Review labor content and judge whether it should go to a low-cost labor region.

5. ZIP design for manufacturer.

6. Controlled product introduction.

7. Market audit and begin again.

Truly remain "continually dissatisfied" with your products and performance. The last famous words of a company failing are, "We have always done it that way."

If you always do what you've always done, you'll always get what you've always gotten.

MANUFACTURING STRATEGY DEVELOPMENT … THE PROCESS

OVERVIEW:

This workshop facilitates the evolution of "CDA," Competitive Design Assessment, to a conclusive plan which provides the manufacturer of a competitive manufacturing plan based on the manufacturer's "Vision."

Craig Offutt

Week 1: Team & DMC
3 Day - 2 Homework Sessions

- Establish Conclusive Vision
- Functional Wish List
- Business Status & Analysis

Week 2: DMC

DMC Site Review, Data Collection
& Development Of Information Base

Week 3: Team & DMC
4 - 5 Day Workshop

DFMA Re-Design ... "Big Picture
Projection

Week 4: DMC

Re-Design Summary & Projected
Approach

Week 5: Team & DMC
3 Day Session

Re-Design Review: Manufacturing
Alternative Development

Week 6 & 7: DMC

- Site Work Detail
- Investment Projection
- Capacity Reviews

Week 8: Team & DMC
4 Day Session

- Final Strategy Development
- Next Steps
- Summary

The Process Can Extend Up To 12 Weeks Depending Upon The Accumulation Of Data !!

66

Chapter Nine
Customer Response

This chapter is short and sweet. It does not take a rocket scientist to figure out whether you did your job or not. If the product does not sell, then you misfired on the market, did not do your competitive analysis correctly, or you are not getting proper market exposure.

I do not claim to be an expert in advertising, just an expert in new product delivery at best cost. Given that you were selling products before and that your system was working it should mean that you misfired.

A perfect example is the minivan. Ford did a review a few years ago and from their market research decided that the consumer was not interested in double sliding doors. So, they tooled the Aerostar without the option for sliding doors on both the passenger and the driver side. During this same model introduction year, Chrysler's market research not only decided that double sliders should be an option, but that it could become the standard. Therefore, they needed a contingency plan to be able to produce minivans with 100% double sliders. The end result is that Ford had to re-tool at a significant cost and loss of market.

If you are careful and methodical about applying ZIP, recognize that your company has paradigms which would cause failure, then you should be able to anticipate market response. If you do not follow the process and assume you know the market and your competitor, assume that you know what you are doing (because you have always done it that way), you are sure to eventually fail. No competition today gives you the opportunity to get way ahead and protect your business. Do not become complacent until someone decides to steal your business. It is real hard to fix it once you are under those pressures. There is no substitute for planning and execution.

The process of ZIP uses proven technologies applied in a process. If followed with rigor and made a way of life in your company it assures you the ability to overcome the natural adversities of business. Does this strategic logic always work? Yes! Do companies always believe it will work? No! And why not? Because logic is not always logical to the individuals. Remember we have been trained as managers, not leaders, not masters of logic and strategy, but masters of control, auditing and clerking.

Everything in the world, which gets done, should have value. The value may be difficult at times to define but there is value or you should not do it. To redesign a product without increased sales, higher profits, better quality, or higher safety reduction, or some recognizable value would be absurd. Define the value in the beginning and you will not have to worry about market response. Proceed on gut feelings and mark your death, maybe not today, but guaranteed sometime tomorrow.

If your leader lacks vision–fire him. If you lack vision–go hire it or buy it. If you do not recognize that you have it or you do not, go to work for someone else.

ZIP works!

Chapter Ten
Mexican Strategy

DMC has done extensive work in Mexico helping Mexican companies improve, as well as U.S. companies relocate designs, implement and start designs, and introduce them to production. We have an established corporation in Mexico and use it as the focus for this work.

I have stories about the cultural differences that I could write an entire novel on, but I won't. I do not contend that I understand Mexican culture to its detail, but I do understand the things that work and the things that do not.

Inherently, there are some basic business cultures that exist in both countries–Mexico and the U.S. In this chapter, I hope to provide some insight which would help anyone operate in Mexico.

THE BIG 10 GRINGO LESSONS

1. Always be courteous and respectful. Mexicans tend to want to build friendships first and then do business. There is an underlying lack of trust if you are not friends–amigos. Spend time on a personal basis to get to know them and the culture.

2. Be patient. It takes time to develop a relationship and therefore makes the process much slower than in the U.S.

3. Language barriers exist everywhere. If you do not speak Spanish, then learn some and remember that not all words translate. A guy in Italy, who spoke three languages fluently, once said, "In this meeting we speak English, which is your primary language.

I am French, so I have to translate each word mentally while in the conversation." This means that you have all the power. Therefore, make pictures and so on to confirm agreements, and be sure to summarize results for final agreement. Sometimes a signature on a final agreement will make sure that both Gringos and Mexicans agree and understand. Spanish is also 30% longer than English so speak clear, slow and forget the slang. Keep in mind that when they translate they do it literally. Do not use jargon or slang and try to be precise about what you want when you speak.

4. "Manana" translates to "tomorrow" in English. In business, it usually means sometime later and not necessarily tomorrow.

5. Often you hear Gringos say that the Mexicans lied to them or did not meet their commitments. Usually this is untrue. It is due to lack of communications, not a lie. Make sure at the end of a review that there is joint agreement.

6. Things, by nature, move much slower in Mexico. Plan ahead and make sure that everyone understands what the event and actions are before beginning or you will suffer the consequences of delays. Mexican contractors and suppliers tend to promise the world and then fail to deliver on time. Plan on having to follow up on details and have plenty of meetings to make sure all involved know what is happening.

7. If you are not on the job location in Mexico frequently, then you can expect that they will sometimes renege on the agreements. They do not really renege as we know it, but if things happen, they do change their minds without calling for

agreement. Check in frequently to make sure things are going according to plan.

8. When working in a business organization, remember that culturally Mexicans will do whatever the boss says. So, if it is incorrect, you will need to bring it up and get it clarified.

9. Financial measurements are different in Mexico. The way assets and depreciation are handled for tax purposes are significantly different. Make sure you understand these differences and do not make assumptions.

10. Remember that in Mexico and South America they do not have unemployment wages or subsidies. When they are poor, they are poor. Be empathetic to the situation.

THE BIG 10 MEXICAN LESSONS:

1. If you have difficulty with English and do not understand, be sure to tell the Gringos and make them show you or write it down. Remind them to slow down their speech since Spanish is longer and slower.

2. When making an agreement, be sure to meet the specified dates and do not change the agreement without review with the Gringos.

3. Remember that things move faster in the States, so be patient with the Gringos when they tend to get upset or impatient with the situation. Remind them where they are and how things work.

4. If you do not speak English you are in trouble. Gringos tend to be selfish and expect everyone else

to learn their language. It is not right–just the way it is. Learn English. More and more Americans are learning Spanish, but it takes time to change.

5.   Expect to have to supply completion dates and meet your commitments. Come to meetings prepared and try not to meet all day.

6.   Gringos start work earlier and finish work earlier than Mexicans. It's the same with breakfast, lunch and dinner. If you normally eat lunch at 2:00 P.M., and they normally eat at noon, compromise and eat at 1:00 P.M. Do the same for breakfast and dinner. This way both of your time clocks are adjusting.

7.   Financial measurements are different in Mexico, and the way assets and depreciation are handled are different from that of the U.S. Learn the differences and do not make assumptions.

8.   Encourage people from the U.S. to do business the Mexican way and prevent delays and other issues.

9.   Understand that abruptness is acceptable in U.S. business. So, get a little thicker skin and do not take offense to issues.

10. Go to the States and spend some time with the business associates to help you better understand the cultural differences.

The Big 10 Lessons will help both Mexicans and Gringos work more efficiently. I expect that over the next decade the course of business will continue to relocate manufacturing to low-cost labor regions. Twenty years ago, before NAFTA, the movement to Mexico in size began. In more recent times, the crusade is to move lower-level commodity products from Mexico to China and relocate more products from the U.S.

to Mexico. It is a flowing business in the world economy. As Mexico becomes more affluent, and wages rise, some products will need to relocate to other lower labor regions, such as China and Africa.

While we have worked for years in Mexico we learn new skills and cultures almost daily. We find that our clients have very little empathy for the cultural differences and tend to believe that they can do business any way they wish. It is a big mistake! It slows down progress and leaves a poor business relationship between the Gringos and the Mexicans involved.

We have a corporation in Mexico, and when establishing such, it requires significant forethought. When you prepare a charter for incorporation you need to be sure and make the scope large enough that it covers anything that you might vaguely want to do, or you will need to submit for additions and changes. While under current Mexican law you are allowed to establish a 100% foreign-held corporation, the initial incorporation is reasonably simple and inexpensive. Revisions and changes are bureaucratic. If you think the U.S. has red tape, Mexico is worse and less automated.

One of our clients, a large manufacturer with several locations in Mexico and a joint venture with a U.S. firm, was determined that they knew how to do business better than the joint venture Gringo company. As a result there was constant pressure to get the entire Gringo contingent out of the facilities and handle the projects with all Mexicans. While a joint effort is required, many older Mexican managers have great pride in what they can do and like to show the U.S. that they are just as capable, or even better. These are old paradigms. In addition, due to the fact that Mexico had not been turning out as many college degreed people until the last decade, a lot of the upper management is uneducated. All of this is progressively changing. As the educational base continues to grow in Mexico and the number of people increases in this category, the narrower the gap will become between Gringos and Mexicans.

As a result I threatened the client with failure and we agreed to disagree. They maintained my people to support them, but removed me from the leadership role. My point is that if you cannot get agreement of what leadership is in power, then plan to fail. I elected to make one last try at the risk of losing my position. I lost ….

I have always considered it more important to have a successful project than to worry about the lost fees. In my business, success brings new business, failure brings nothing.

I always said that I could write a book about all of the crazy stuff that goes on in Mexican business, but that is not the point of this story. The point is, use the Big 10 Lessons like law and keep your Mexican working career flowing.

Chapter Eleven
The End

We have reached the end of the journey in discussing the ZIP Business Strategy. I hope that I kept my promise and kept the book flowing and interesting.

ZIP is a leadership strategy. Use it, apply it, and treat it as a way of life and you will win. I spent my entire life in business working on this process, utilizing it in hundreds of projects for over 30 years. Only once did I have a project fail. That project did not need to fail and was truly caused by a few Mexicans' desire to oust Gringos from their business.

Use ZIP as your business strategy process and expect to be an Industry World Class leader.

About the Author

Craig R. Offutt, President *DMC* CEO C&C Concerns, Inc.

Craig has a solid background, with focus in the technical disciplines as well as operations and general management. He started as an engineer with a major appliance manufacturer and progressed through the design disciplines over a period of six years. Although by education he is an Electronics Engineer with an MBA, his design background spans from electronics to plastic components.

Craig has spent 17 years in various operations' assignments progressing through management from Quality Design, Quality Assurance, Manufacturing Engineering, Materials, MIS, Maintenance, Tooling, DFM, and Business Strategy Development. These assignments resulted in several factory master plans, several business strategies, new plant start-ups, plant shutdowns and significant mega project implementations.

Wanting to obtain a true business experience with P & L responsibilities, Craig accepted a contract offer to help a small HVAC manufacturer do a financial turnaround. Following the turnaround, Craig recognized that his real strengths were in problem solving and he started the development of the new company.

Based on his experience, Craig wanted to provide services to companies in a consulting role from a productive aspect and not one where the consultant tells you what you already know. Hence, the birth of Design & Manufacturing Consultants.